Dedicated to all the

TROUSER TRUMPETERS

out there!

We salute you

My Mum is fantastic.
She really is the best.

She is great at lots of things, much better than the rest.

There is just one thing, which makes me quite mad.

That is, when it comes to keeping her farts in, she really is very bad!

She loves to let rip all day long...

At home, at work, always letting out a pong.

It's especially awful when we are in the car.

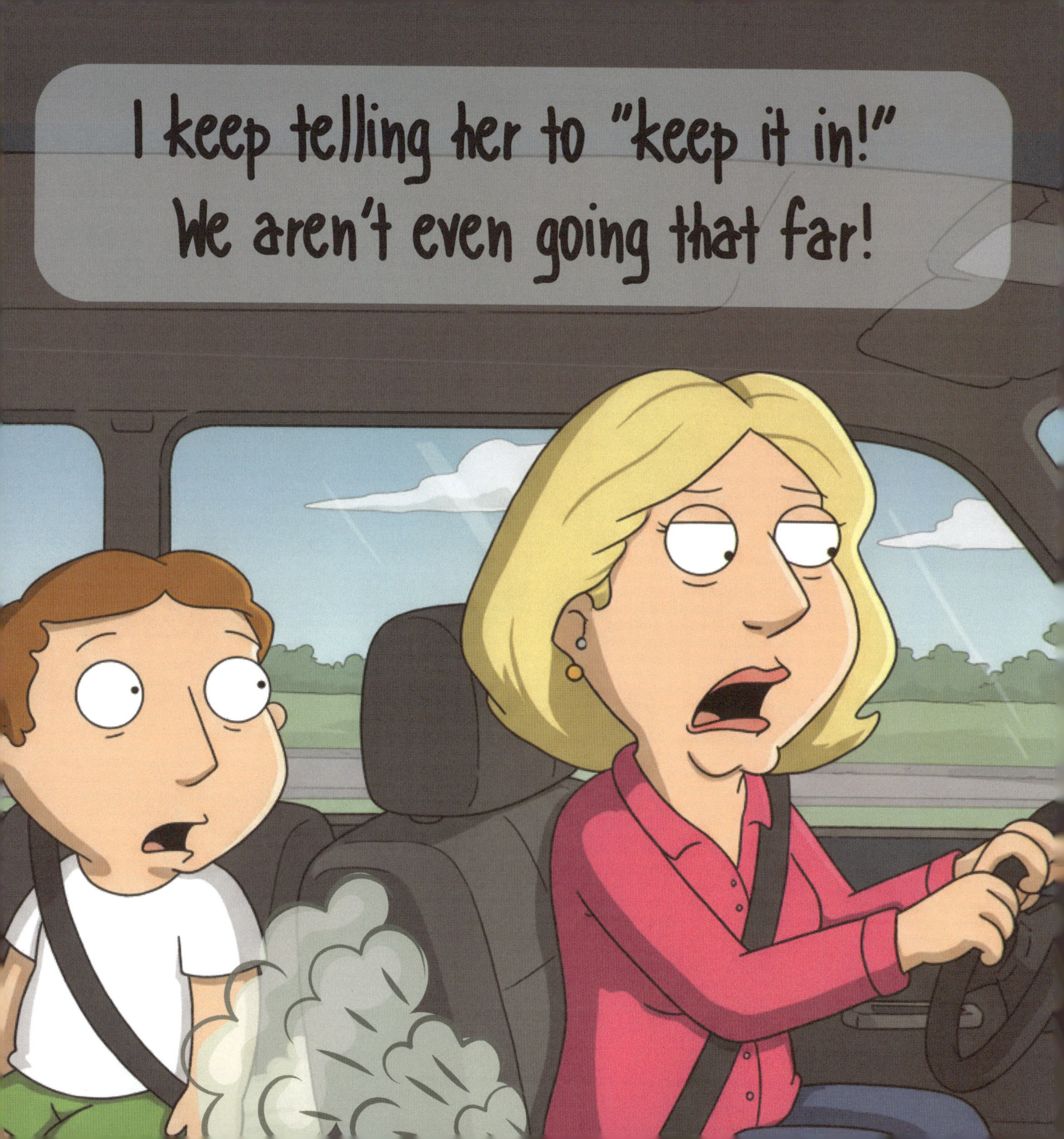
I keep telling her to "keep it in!"
We aren't even going that far!

My friends think it's funny.
They laugh all the time.
They wish they could have a Mum like mine.

I really do love my Mum,
But I just get so embarrassed,
by her noisy bum.

That is until one day, Mum's bum took all the glory.

It was amazing!
Let me tell you the story…

They were building a rocket to send to the moon.

But, try as they might, they couldn't make it go zoom!

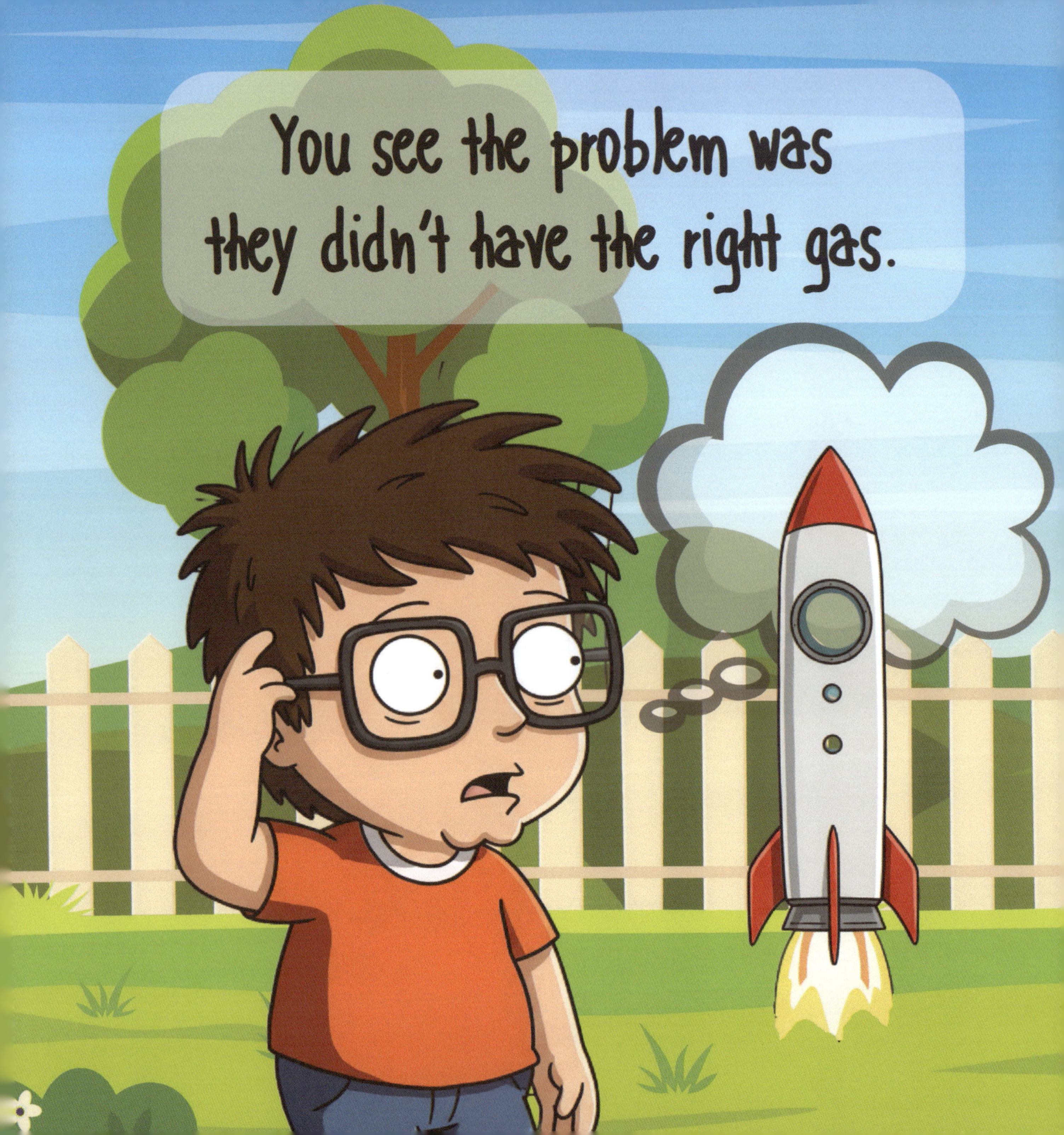
You see the problem was
they didn't have the right gas.

They didn't have enough power to make it go fast.

They tried and tried many a different thing.

But, none of it worked, to make it spring.

When Mum seen the news, she knew she had the power.

She started planning how to save the hour.

So, Mum built herself a pair of trumpet trousers.

Something to make the crowd say "Wowsers!"

Then Mum confidently shouted "I have the power to send this rocket soaring!"

Step back everyone, "This is not going to be boring!"

Mum's Trumpet Trousers were connected to the rocket's windpipe.

Then out came a noise that gave everyone a fright.

Mum's bum EXPLODED with an almighty roar!

And up went the rocket!
Higher and higher we watched it soar.

The crowd cheered, "Hip Hip Hooray!"

Mum's Trumpet Trousers have saved the day.

HOORAY FOR TRUMPET TROUSERS!

FART POWER RULES!

And now, I couldn't be more proud,
Whenever Mum's bum erupts and it is loud.

I no longer mind. No, I really don't care. Whenever people gasp or stop and stare.

When I grow up I want to be just like her, you see.

Letting farts rip and setting them free!

Printed in Great Britain
by Amazon